VOCAL SELECTIONS
from

Music by **HAROLD ARLEN** • Lyrics by **E. Y. HARBURG**

T0087370

Contents

7182

44116

FROM THE MUSICAL PRODUCTION "JAMAICA"

PUSH DE BUTTON

Lyric by
E. Y. HARBURG

Music by
HAROLD ARLEN

There's a lit-tle is-land on the Hud-son, myth-i-cal mag-ic and fair;

shin-ing like a dia-mon' on de Hud-son, far a-way from wor-ri-ment and care. What an

isle, what an isle, all the na-tives re-lax there in style. What a life, what a

FROM THE MUSICAL PRODUCTION "JAMAICA"

COCOANUT SWEET

Lyric by
E. Y. HARBURG

Music by
HAROLD ARLEN

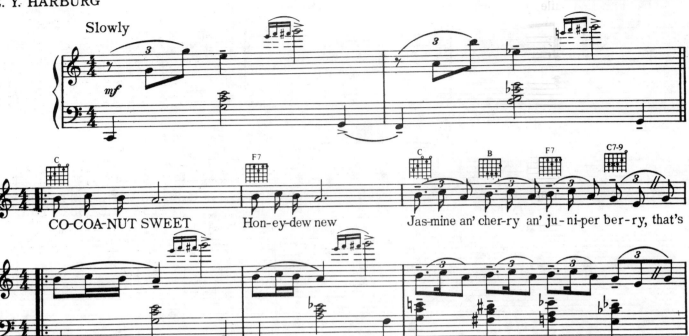

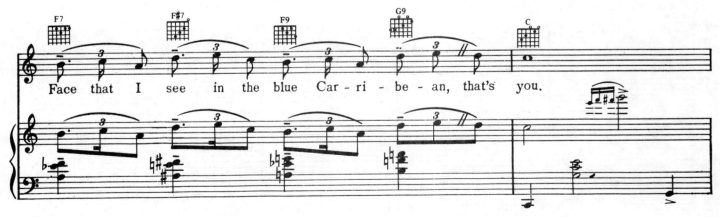

CO-COA-NUT SWEET Hon-ey-dew new Jas-mine an' cher-ry an' ju-ni-per ber-ry, that's

you. CO-COA-NUT SWEET But-ter-cup true

Face that I see in the blue Car-ri-be-an, that's you.

LITTLE BISCUIT

Lyric by
E. Y. HARBURG

Music by
HAROLD ARLEN

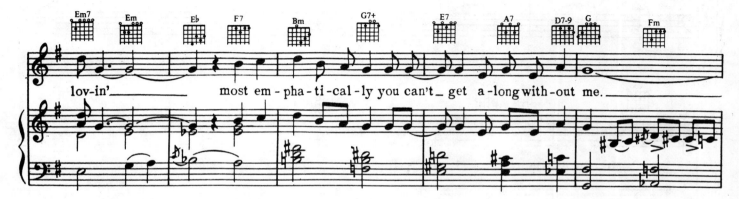

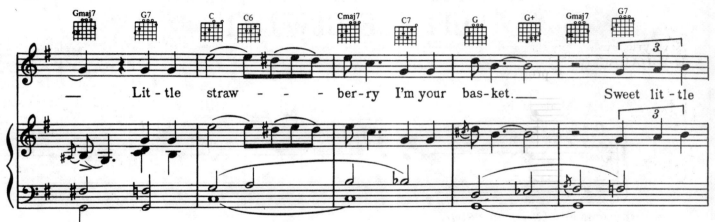

Lit-tle straw - - - ber-ry I'm your bas-ket. Sweet lit-tle

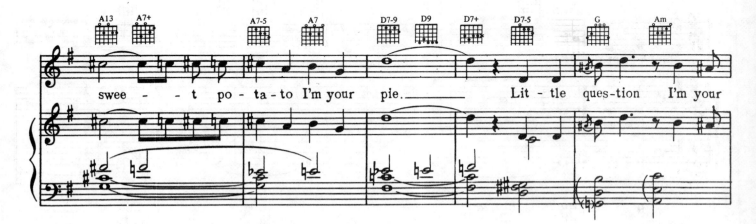

swee - t po-ta-to I'm your pie. Lit-tle ques-tion I'm your

an-swer if you ask it. Lit-tle moon-stone,

lit-tle dia-mon', I won't stop this cra-zy rhy-min', 'till you and me are co-

mun - i - ty prop - er - ty. _____ Like it read in the book __

__ like it sing in the song ____ you ca - n't get a -

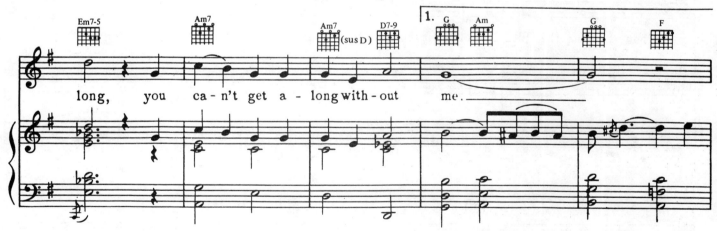

long, you ca - n't get a - long with - out me. _____

1.

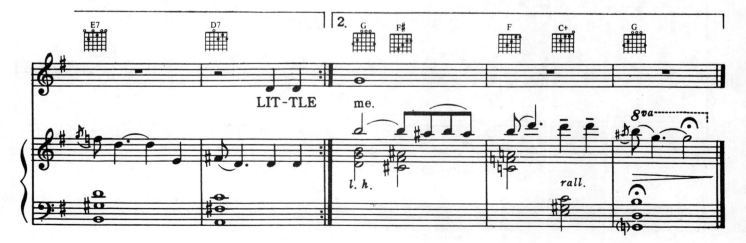

2. LIT - TLE me.

FROM THE MUSICAL PRODUCTION "JAMAICA"

I DON'T THINK I'LL END IT ALL TODAY

Lyric by
E. Y. HARBURG

Music by
HAROLD ARLEN

Playfully

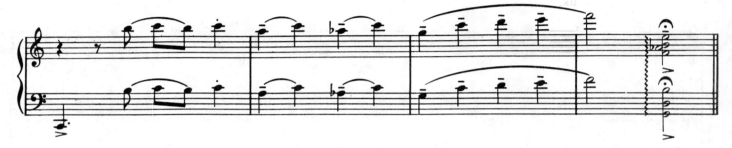

Voice

When I hear the lilt___ of your laugh-ter what is there to say.

I don't think, oh no,___ I DON'T THINK, I'LL END IT ALL TO-DAY.

FROM THE MUSICAL PRODUCTION "JAMAICA"

SAVANNA

Lyric by
E. Y. HARBURG

Music by
HAROLD ARLEN

FROM THE MUSICAL PRODUCTION "JAMAICA"

TAKE IT SLOW, JOE

Lyric by
E. Y. HARBURG

Music by
HAROLD ARLEN

FROM THE MUSICAL PRODUCTION "JAMAICA"

WHAT GOOD DOES IT DO?

Lyric by
E.Y. HARBURG

Music by
HAROLD ARLEN

Slowly, Blues

De sun is full o' li-quor, De

earth is full o' wine, Crick-ets do-in' nip-ups 'Round de col-um-bine.

De

feel-in' is in-fec-tious, June is ev-'ry-where, Hearts light and wind-y

FROM THE MUSICAL PRODUCTION "JAMAICA"

PRETTY TO WALK WITH
(That's How A Man Gets Got)

Lyric by
E. Y. HARBURG

Music by
HAROLD ARLEN

FROM THE MUSICAL PRODUCTION "JAMAICA"

NAPOLEON

Lyric by
E.Y. HARBURG

Music by
HAROLD ARLEN

NA-PO-LE-ON'S a pas-try _____ Get this un-der your
Hom-er is just a swat_ King John a you-know-what_ Get this un-der your

brow, what once_ us-ta_ be a_ roos-ter_ is just_
brow, all these_ big wheel_ con-tra - ver-cials are just_

_ a dus-ter now_
_ com-mer-cials now_

NA-PO-LE-ON'S a pas-try_

Bet-ter get your jug of wine and

loaf of love be-fore that fi-nal bow _____